1. Cape May Bird Observatory – Northwood Center
2. Cape May Bird Observatory – Center for Research and Education
3. Avalon Seawatch – Cape May Bird Observatory
4. Cape May National Wildlife Refuge
5. Stone Harbor Bird Sanctuary
6. Cape May Wetlands State Natural Area
7. South Cape May Meadows
8. New Jersey Birding and Wildlife Trails
9. The Wetlands Institute
10. Morning Flight Songbird Count – Cape May Observatory, Higbee Beach
11. Stainton Wildlife Refuge
12. NJA Hovnanian Sanctuary
13. New Jersey Audubon's Scherman Hoffman Wildlife Sanctuary
14. Hawk Rise Sanctuary
15. Nessie Bog Birdwatching Area
16. Richard W. DeKorte Park
17. The Celery Farm (Wetlands Preserve)
18. Charles H. Rogers Wildlife Refuge
19. Island Beach State Park
20. Great Swamp National Wildlife Refuge
21. Sandy Hook
22. Forsythe National Wildlife Refuge
23. Barnegat Light State Park

Most illustrations show the adult male in breeding coloration. Colors and markings may be duller or absent during different seasons. The measurements denote the length of most species from nose/bill to tail tip. Illustrations are not to scale.

Waterford Press publishes reference guides that introduce readers to nature observation, outdoor recreation and survival skills. Product information is featured on the website: www.waterfordpress.com

Text & illustrations © 2022 Waterford Press Inc. All rights reserved. Photos © Shutterstock. To order or for information on custom published products please call 800-434-2555 or email orderdesk@waterfordpress.com. For permissions or to share comments email editor@waterfordpress.com

978-1-62005-509-0 $7.95 U.S.
Made in the USA

NEW JERSEY SHOREBIRDS

ATLANTIC OCEAN

A Waterproof Folding Guide to Familiar Species

Kavanagh/Leung

NEW JERSEY SHOREBIRDS

Common Loon
Gavia immer
To 3 ft. (90 cm)
Haunting call sounds like – yodel-ha-oo-oo.

Winter / Summer

Red-throated Loon
Gavia stellata
To 25 in. (63 cm)

Horned Grebe
Podiceps auritus
To 15 in. (38 cm)

Pied-billed Grebe
Podilymbus podiceps
To 13 in. (33 cm)
Note banded white bill.

Snow Goose
Chen caerulescens
To 31 in. (78 cm)

Brant
Branta bernicla
To 26 in. (65 cm)
Note white neck mark.

Canada Goose
Branta canadensis
To 45 in. (1.4 m)

Mute Swan
Cygnus olor To 5 ft. (1.5 m)
Introduced resident species.

Northern Pintail
Anas acuta To 30 in. (75 cm)
Male is distinguished by its long tail, brown head and white neck. Both have a dark speculum and a white belly.

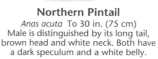

Wood Duck
Aix sponsa To 20 in. (50 cm)
Males have strikingly colorful plumage and a distinctive, dark crest. Note the white neck bridle.

Green-winged Teal
Anas crecca To 16 in. (40 cm)
The smallest of the dabbling ducks. The species is named for the green speculum visible in flight.

Blue-winged Teal
Anas discors To 16 in. (40 cm)
Male's white facial crescent is distinctive. Female has spotted sides. Note blue forewing in flight.

Mallard
Anas platyrhynchos To 26 in. (65 cm)
Male has metallic green head and chestnut breast. Blue speculum has white borders.

American Black Duck
Anas rubripes To 25 in. (63 cm)
Black-brown duck has a pale head and neck. Speculum is violet and undersides of wings are white. Sexes are similar.

Lesser Scaup
Aythya affinis To 18 in. (45 cm)
Note peaked crown. White wing patch is shorter than greater scaup's. Color is not a reliable way to distinguish scaups.

Redhead
Aythya americana To 22 in. (55 cm)
Note rounded head. Female has a light eye ring. Summers on inland lakes and ponds, and winters along the coast.

Ring-necked Duck
Aythya collaris To 18 in. (45 cm)
Note white ring near bill tip. Male also has a white ring at the bill base. Females have a light eye ring and stripe extending back from eye.

Greater Scaup
Aythya marila To 20 in. (50 cm)
Note rounded head and long white wing stripe in flight. Note white patch at base of female's bill.

Canvasback
Aythya valisineria To 2 ft. (60 cm)
Note sloping forehead and black bill. Male has a chestnut head; female's is pale brown.

Bufflehead
Bucephala albeola To 15 in. (38 cm)
Males and females both have a large, puffy head and short bill. Note the black face and white head patch of males.

Common Goldeneye
Bucephala clangula To 18 in. (45 cm)
Male has a white facial spot. Note the tapered forehead and long bill with yellow tip.

Long-tailed Duck
Clangula hyemalis To 22 in. (55 cm)
Only males have the long, wispy tail feathers that give this species its common name. Call resembles a loud warble.

Harlequin Duck
Histrionicus histrionicus To 17 in. (43 cm)
Note steep forehead and long tail. Male plumage is distinctive although it appears dark at a distance. Female has three white head spots.

Hooded Merganser
Lophodytes cucullatus To 20 in. (50 cm)
Male is told by white head crest and thin bill. Female has a puffy brownish head crest.

American Wigeon
Mareca americana To 23 in. (58 cm)
Breeding males have a distinctive bright white crown and an iridescent green swoosh behind the eye. Flocks congregate in lakes, ponds, and fields.

Gadwall
Mareca strepera To 23 in. (58 cm)
Male has grey body and black rear. Both sexes have a white belly.

Black Scoter
Melanitta americana To 20 in. (50 cm)
Black male has orangish knob on its bill. Female's pale face contrasts its dark crown and body.

White-winged Scoter
Melanitta deglandi To 23 in. (58 cm)
Note white wing patches that are especially conspicuous in flight. Male has a white eye patch; female has white facial patches.

Surf Scoter
Melanitta perspicillata To 20 in. (50 cm)
Black male has white patches on nape and forehead and a multi-colored bill. Female has two white cheek patches.

Common Merganser
Mergus merganser To 27 in. (68 cm)
A breeding male's dark green head contrasts with its mainly white body plumage. Note thin red bill.

Red-breasted Merganser
Mergus serrator To 27 in. (68 cm)
Note thin bill and prominent head crest. Common in coastal areas during winter.

Ruddy Duck
Oxyura jamaicensis To 16 in. (40 cm)
Note broad bill. Tail is often cocked in the air when swimming.

Common Eider
Somateria mollissima To 28 in. (70 cm)
Diving duck common on rocky shorelines and bay shallows. Note sloping head profile.

Northern Shoveler
Spatula clypeata To 20 in. (50 cm)
Named for its broad, shovel-shaped bill. Note the male's reddish-brown sides.

American Coot
Fulica americana
To 16 in. (40 cm)

Clapper Rail
Rallus longirostris
To 16 in. (40 cm)

Double-crested Cormorant
Phalacrocorax auritus
To 3 ft. (90 cm)

Glossy Ibis
Plegadis falcinellus
To 26 in. (65 cm)

Great Blue Heron
Ardea herodias
To 4.5 ft. (1.4 m)

Green Heron
Butorides virescens
To 22 in. (55 cm)

Black-crowned Night-Heron
Nycticorax nycticorax
To 28 in. (70 cm)

Great Egret
Ardea alba
To 38 in. (95 cm)
Note yellow bill and black feet.

Little Blue Heron
Egretta caerulea
To 2 ft. (60 cm)
Note maroon neck.

Snowy Egret
Egretta thula
To 26 in. (65 cm)
Note black bill and yellow feet.

American Oystercatcher
Haematopus palliatus

Piping Plover
Charadrius melodus
To 7 in. (18 cm)
Endangered.

Black-bellied Plover
Pluvialis squatarola
To 14 in. (35 cm)

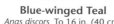

Whimbrel
Numenius phaeopus
To 20 in. (50 cm)
Note striped crown.

Red-necked Phalarope
Phalaropus lobatus
To 8 in. (20 cm)
Female is larger and more colorful than the male.

Dovekie
Alle alle
To 9 in. (23 cm)

Willet
Tringa semipalmata
To 17 in. (43 cm)
Wings flash black-and-white in flight.

Greater Yellowlegs
Tringa melanoleuca
To 15 in. (38 cm)
Call is a 3-5 note whistle.

Lesser Yellowlegs
Tringa flavipes
To 10 in. (25 cm)

American Woodcock
Scolopax minor
To 12 in. (30 cm)
Chunky, long-billed bird.

Killdeer
Charadrius vociferus
To 12 in. (30 cm)
Note two breast bands.

Wilson's Snipe
Gallinago delicata
To 12 in. (30 cm)

Red Knot
Calidris canutus
To 12 in. (30 cm)
Plump, red-breasted shorebird.

Dunlin
Calidris alpina
To 9 in. (23 cm)
Note black belly patch.

Ruddy Turnstone
Arenaria interpres
To 10 in. (25 cm)

Semipalmated Sandpiper
Calidris pusilla
To 7 in. (18 cm)

Purple Sandpiper
Calidris maritima
To 9 in. (23 cm)

Sanderling
Calidris alba
To 8 in. (20 cm)
Runs in and out with waves along shorelines.

Atlantic Puffin
Fratercula arctica
To 12 in. (30 cm)

Common Murre
Uria aalge
To 17 in. (43 cm)

Herring Gull
Larus argentatus
To 26 in. (65 cm)
Wing tips are black with white spots. Legs are pinkish.

Ring-billed Gull
Larus delawarensis
To 20 in. (50 cm)
Bill has dark ring.

Great Black-backed Gull
Larus marinus
To 32 in. (80 cm)
Told by large size and dark back.

Laughing Gull
Leucophaeus atricilla
To 18 in. (45 cm)

Common Tern
Sterna hirundo
To 15 in. (38 cm)
Note black cap and forked tail. Orange bill is black-tipped.

Black Skimmer
Rynchops niger
To 20 in. (50 cm)
Feeds by skimming over water with its lower bill cutting the water's surface to spear fish.

Forster's Tern
Sterna forsteri
To 15 in. (38 cm)
Note forked tail and white wing tips.

Bridled Tern
Onychoprion anaethetus
To 15 in. (38 cm)

Audubon's Shearwater
Puffinus lherminieri
To 12 in. (30 cm)

Manx Shearwater
Puffinus puffinus
To 10 in. (25 cm)

Northern Fulmar
Fulmarus glacialis
To 18 in. (45 cm)
Ocean glider has a stubby yellow bill with tubelike nostrils.

Leach's Storm-Petrel
Oceanodroma leucorhoa
To 8 in. (20 cm)
Note white rump and light bars on upperwings.

Band-rumped Storm-Petrel
Oceanodroma castro
To 8 in. (20 cm)

Northern Gannet
Morus bassanus
To 40 in. (1 m)
Large white sea bird has black wing tips.

Long-tailed Jaeger
Stercorarius longicaudus
To 2 ft. (60 cm)
Arctic breeder regularly winters in the Antarctic.

Pomarine Skua
Stercorarius pomarinus To 26 in. (65 cm)
Note yellowish neck and elongated tail streamer.

Rock Pigeon
Columba livia
To 13 in. (33 cm)
Common in urban areas.

Mourning Dove
Zenaida macroura
To 13 in. (33 cm)

Yellow-billed Cuckoo
Coccyzus americanus
To 14 in. (35 cm)

Ruby-throated Hummingbird
Archilochus colubris
To 3.5 in. (9 cm)

Belted Kingfisher
Megaceryle alcyon
To 14 in. (35 cm)

Northern Bobwhite
Colinus virginianus
To 12 in. (30 cm)

Whip-poor-will
Antrostomus vociferus
To 10 in. (25 cm)
Its rhythmic call – whip-poor-will – can be heard at night.

Chuck-will's-widow
Antrostomus carolinensis
To 12 in. (30 cm)

Chimney Swift
Chaetura pelagica
To 6 in. (15 cm)

Common Nighthawk
Chordeiles minor
To 10 in. (25 cm)
Often hunts for insects around street lights.

Downy Woodpecker
Dryobates pubescens
To 6 in. (15 cm)
The similar hairy woodpecker is larger and has a longer bill.

Red-bellied Woodpecker
Melanerpes carolinus
To 11 in. (28 cm)

Northern Flicker
Colaptes auratus
To 13 in. (33 cm)
Wing and tail linings are yellow.

Black Vulture
Coragyps atratus
To 27 in. (68 cm)
Black head is bald.

Turkey Vulture
Cathartes aura
To 32 in. (80 cm)
Note red head and two-toned underwings.

Osprey
Pandion haliaetus
To 2 ft. (60 cm)
Fish-eating raptor is often seen perched along lakes and rivers.

Bald Eagle
Haliaeetus leucocephalus
To 40 in. (1 m)

Northern Harrier
Circus hudsonius
To 22 in. (55 cm)
Note V-shaped flight profile and white rump.

Sharp-shinned Hawk
Accipiter striatus
To 14 in. (35 cm)
Note long, square-edged tail and striped breast.

Cooper's Hawk
Accipiter cooperii
To 20 in. (50 cm)
Note long, rounded white-tipped tail.

Light Morph

Red-tailed Hawk
Buteo jamaicensis
To 25 in. (63 cm)
Tail has a rufous wash.

Rough-legged Hawk
Buteo lagopus
To 2 ft. (60 cm)
Note dark 'wrists'.

Red-shouldered Hawk
Buteo lineatus
To 22 in. (55 cm)
Note reddish shoulder patches and rust underparts.

Broad-winged Hawk
Buteo platypterus
To 19 in. (48 cm)
Note dark and light tail bands.

Merlin
Falco columbarius
To 14 in. (35 cm)
Note small size. Tail is heavily banded.

Peregrine Falcon
Falco peregrinus
To 20 in. (50 cm)
Note dark 'mustache'.

American Kestrel
Falco sparverius
To 12 in. (30 cm)

Great Horned Owl
Bubo virginianus
To 25 in. (63 cm)
Call is a resonant – hoo-HOO-hoooo.

Barred Owl
Strix varia
To 2 ft. (60 cm)
Call is a loud – who-cooks-for-you? who-cooks-for-you-all?

Eastern Screech-Owl
Megascops asio
To 9 in. (23 cm)
Small owl with yellow eyes. Color varies.

American Crow
Corvus brachyrhynchos
To 22 in. (55 cm)
Call is a distinct – caw.

Fish Crow
Corvus ossifragus
To 20 in. (50 cm)
Call is a short nasal – ca.

Boat-tailed Grackle
Quiscalus major
To 16 in. (40 cm)
Long tail is keel-shaped.

Red-winged Blackbird
Agelaius phoeniceus
To 9 in. (23 cm)

Cedar Waxwing
Bombycilla cedrorum
To 7 in. (18 cm)
Red wing marks look like waxy droplets.

Yellow-rumped Warbler
Setophaga coronata
To 6 in. (15 cm)
Note yellow on rump and crown and white throat.

Cape May Warbler
Setophaga tigrina
To 5 in. (13 cm)
Note chestnut cheek.

Swamp Sparrow
Melospiza georgiana
To 6 in. (15 cm)
Note red cap and white throat.

Seaside Sparrow
Ammodramus maritimus
To 6 in. (15 cm)

White-crowned Sparrow
Zonotrichia leucophrys
To 8 in. (20 cm)
White crown is bordered by black stripes.

White-throated Sparrow
Zonotrichia albicollis
To 7 in. (18 cm)

Slate-colored Race

Dark-eyed Junco
Junco hyemalis
To 7 in. (18 cm)

House Sparrow
Passer domesticus
To 6 in. (15 cm)